To
Johnny Adams —

Enjoy!

 Ross Winters '91

A TASTE OF CARMEL

RECIPES BY CARMEL'S TOP CHEFS

PORTRAITS BY BILL BATES

TEXT BY MARIE WILSON

© **1990 Marie Wilson and Bill Bates**
All rights reserved. No part of this publication may be
reproduced in any form without permission from the authors.

ISBN 0-9588566-5-6

Printed in Hong Kong

Published by:
A TASTE OF CARMEL
Marie Wilson and Bill Bates
P.O. Box 2213
Carmel-by-the-Sea, California 93921
(408) 624-4890

Contents

Anton & Michel 5

Casa Bella 9

Casanova 13

Chutneys 15

The Covey 19

Flaherty's 23

The French Poodle 27

Friar Tuck's 31

Giuliano's 33

La Boheme 37

Pacific's Edge 41

Raffaello 45

Rio Grill 47

Robata Grill 51

Sans Souci 53

Spyglass 57

Tuck Box 61

Jai Lal

Anton & Michel

What distinguishes this place from others is a lovely courtyard setting where one can dine indoors or outside by the fountain. Anton & Michel opened their fine restaurant almost a dozen years ago. Michel Nazzal is abroad now in his native country of Jordan, and cousin Anton Salameh, or Tony as he is known by his clientele, presides over the day-to-day operations. In the kitchen is found chef Jai Lal, originally from the Fiji Islands. Lal apprenticed at The Lodge at Pebble Beach and Carmel's Pine Inn before joining Anton & Michel, where lamb dishes are his forte. He recommends the rack of lamb for two—one sure thing—those who taste it will return for more!

APPETIZER
Baked Feta In Filo
Serves about three dozen triangles

- 2 cups Feta cheese crumbs
- 1 cup parsley, finely chopped
- 1 onion, finely chopped
- 1/2 pound spinach
- 1/2 cup olive oil
- 1/2 teaspoon sumac
- salt and pepper to taste
- 6 sheets of filo dough
- 1/2 cup butter, melted

Wash spinach, chop and sprinkle with salt. Let stand for 15 minutes then squeeze out excess moisture. Mix above ingredients together and set aside.

Purchase ready-made filo dough. Lay out filo, one sheet at a time. Lightly brush with butter and cut into 3-inch wide strips. Place a heaping teaspoon of filling in one corner and fold over into a triangle. Continue folding until filling is completely encased in filo. Repeat the above procedure until all filling is used up. Place 1 inch apart on ungreased baking sheet. Bake uncovered for 10 minutes in a 375 degree oven or until golden brown. Serve warm.

SOUP
Lentil Soup With Swiss Chard
Serves Four

1-1/2 cups of lentils
1 pound Swiss chard, chopped
1 large onion, chopped
1/4 cup olive oil
1 tablespoon flour
1/2 cup lemon juice
1/2 teaspoon cumin
salt and pepper to taste
6 cups water

Wash lentils thoroughly, place in water and simmer for 30 minutes (covered). Add chopped onions and Swiss chard to the cooking lentils. Cover and simmer for 50 minutes or until tender.

Mix flour with oil, lemon juice, salt and cumin then add to the cooking mixture to thicken the soup. Simmer for a few more minutes and serve hot.

MAIN COURSE
Chicken Jerusalem
Serves Four

4 full breasts of chicken with skin on
10 ounces artichoke hearts, halved
8 ounces mushrooms, quartered
1/4 cup olive oil
1/2 teaspoon thyme (dried and crushed)
1/2 teaspoon oregano (dried and crushed)
1 teaspoon shallots
1 teaspoon garlic
1/2 cup Chardonnay
1 cup heavy cream
salt and ground pepper

Place artichoke hearts in a pot of cold water. Add 1/2 teaspoon of salt. Bring water to a boil then simmer for approximately 10 minutes. Drain and set aside.

Salt and pepper the breast of chicken. Heat the olive oil in a skillet, sauté the chicken until all sides are nice and brown (about 10 minutes on medium heat). Remove chicken from skillet and place in a warm spot. Add garlic, shallots and mushrooms to the skillet. Sauté until mushrooms are half cooked. Deglaze pan with Chardonnay and add the thyme and oregano. Reduce by half then add the artichoke hearts, cream and the chicken. Cook for about 10 minutes on high heat and reduce until sauce is thick. Taste and season accordingly.

DESSERT
Creme Brûlée (Burnt Cream)
Serves Four

- 1-1/2 cups heavy cream
- 1-1/2 cups light cream (half-and-half)
- 4 large egg yolks, well beaten
- 1/3 cup sugar
- 1 teaspoon cornstarch
- 1 teaspoon vanilla or almond extract
- 1/2 cup light brown sugar

Heat mixture of heavy cream and light cream together slowly until a light skin forms on top. Remove from heat. Set aside to cool. Beat eggs and add mixture of sugar and cornstarch gradually while beating constantly. Add cream very slowly while stirring briskly. Return custard mixture to the pan and cook it without allowing it to boil, until it thickens. As soon as the custard coats a metal spoon, remove from heat and stir in almond or vanilla extract. Pour mixture into four individual heatproof dishes (soufflé cups) and refrigerate overnight.

A couple of hours before the meal, sprinkle top of chilled cream with an even layer of brown sugar. Place under broiler until sugar caramelizes.

Marc Vandenhove

Casa Bella

*T*hose who make the drive through beautiful Carmel Valley will be thrilled to dine at Marc Vandenhove's Casa Bella Restaurant in Carmel Valley Village. This Belgian chef/owner gained experience in Europe, Canada, San Francisco and other Carmel restaurants prior to establishing his own Mediterranean-style eatery. What sets this place aside from others is a diverse menu at reasonable prices. It is definitely a worthwhile drive from Carmel.

APPETIZER
Soft Shell Crab
Serves Four

- 4 crabs (soft shell)
- 1 soup spoon pink whole pepper corn
- 1 egg
- 1/2 cup milk
- 1 cup bread crumbs
- salt and pepper
- 1/4 cup chicken stock
- 2 soup spoons white wine
- 1 teaspoon raspberry vinegar
- 2 soup spoons soft butter
- 1 tablespoon butter
- 1 tablespoon olive oil

Beat egg, milk, salt and pepper; dip crab in egg and milk. Cover with bread crumbs. Put 1 tablespoon butter and 1 tablespoon oil in frying pan, heat up high. Sauté the crabs on each side until golden. Set crab on a tray and keep in oven at 350 degrees for 5 minutes.

In frying pan, add pink pepper corn and deglaze with raspberry vinegar. Add white wine and chicken stock. Reduce the sauce by 1/2 volume, remove from heat. Add soft butter, salt and pepper to taste. Pour sauce on plate and place crab on top.

Garnish with fresh basil and one-half lemon.

SALAD

Spinach Salad Arugula
Serves Four

1/2	pound of spinach
6	leaves of arugula
1/2	carrot
1/4	cup raspberry vinegar
2	hard boiled eggs
2	chicken breasts
	olive oil
1/4	cup chicken stock
	butter

Cut chicken in fine strips and sauté in butter. Deglaze pan with raspberry vinegar and chicken stock. Reduce by 1/2 volume. Pour the warm liquid and chicken on the spinach mixed with arugula. Add chopped egg, olive oil, salt and pepper and carrots julienne. Fold gently and serve.

SOUP

Shrimp Bisque

1	large onion
2	stalks celery
1	large carrot
2	tablespoons butter
2	tablespoons olive oil
2	pounds fish bones (rock fish)
6	cups fish stock
3	tablespoons tomato paste
4	cups chopped or diced tomatoes
1	cup white wine
1	teaspoon of fennel seeds
	salt
	pepper (cayenne)
	thyme
2	bay leaves
1/2	cup baby shrimp
1	tablespoon cornstarch
1/4	pint whipping cream

Cut onion, celery and carrots in small cubes. Sauté in butter and oil. Add fish bones. Add tomato paste, chopped tomato with juice and white wine; cover the ingredients with fish stock. Add salt, pepper, thyme, bay leaves and fennel seeds. Cook for one hour. Strain the bisque. Add cream and chopped shrimp and cook for 15 minutes. Dilute cornstarch in liquid. Add gradually until bisque thickens. Garnish with baby shrimp.

MAIN COURSE
Salmon Paillarde Tomatillo Puree
Serves Four

4	salmon steaks, finely sliced
4	tomatillos, chopped
1	juice of lemon
1	cup chicken stock
	salt
	pepper
$1/4$	pound butter

In a roasting pan pour the chopped tomatillos, lemon juice, chicken stock, salt and pepper. Place the salmon on it. Bake in 500 degree oven for 4 minutes. Turn the salmon and finish cooking (about 3 minutes). Display salmon on serving tray or plate. Stir soft butter into sauce. If too thick, add chicken stock for desired consistency.

Serve with small red potatoes, boiled, and sauté green beans with shallots in butter.

DESSERT
Chocolate Mousse

$1/3$	pound dark chocolate
$1/2$	quart whipping cream
3	egg whites
2	tablespoons sugar
1	tablespoon cointreau or triple sec

Melt chocolate with a tablespoon of water over low heat. Whip cream and sugar until the consistency is firm. Whip egg whites until firm. Pour warm chocolate into the whipped cream and mix rapidly. Fold in the egg whites. Add the cointreau and mix gently.

Didier Dutertre

Casanova

*H*oused in a replica of a French farmhouse, this Belgian family-owned restaurant offers an imaginative Mediterranean-style menu. On fine days, the outdoor seating is popular. Chef Didier Dutertre graduated from Ecole Hoteliere de Strasbourg in France. After working in fine restaurants in France, Switzerland and on the French Riviera, he came to Carmel. "I had in mind to stay a year or two," says the Frenchman, "but I met my wife and decided to settle here." Didier has been cooking since he was a youngster. "I liked being around the kitchen and cooking with my grandparents—that's how I got the hang of it." His two-year stay has extended to eight years, during which Chef Dutertre has established a top reputation at the popular restaurant.

MAIN COURSE
Spaghetti "Mimo Di Capri"
Serves Four

- 1 pound spaghetti
- 1 ½ pound beef tip tenderloin (cut into 1/2 inch pieces)
- fresh basil
- 2 diced large tomatoes
- 12 ounces sliced medium mushrooms
- 1 bunch of green onions, chopped
- 8 ounces grated Parmesan cheese
- 32 ounces tomato sauce (homemade or a good quality sauce from a gourmet store)
- olive oil

Cook spaghetti in a large pot of boiling salted water until al dente, drain and cool with cold water.

In a sauté pan, heat up the olive oil. Add the beef tips, sear them very quickly over high heat. Add sliced mushrooms, tomatoes and green onions. Sauté for 2 minutes. Add pre-heated tomato sauce; simmer for 1 minute and add finely chopped fresh basil.

In the meantime, heat up the spaghetti. Divide between 4 large plates. Ladle sauce over spaghetti. Sprinkle with Parmesan cheese and serve.

Fuad Bahou and Debby Corlew

Chutneys

One can never go wrong at this delightful eatery where owners Fuad Bahou and Debby Corlew serve up rich and varied dishes that represent a philosophy of creativity in food preparation. "We believe that nothing affects our mood more directly than food, what we eat, how we eat, when and with whom we eat. The thought of food triggers imagination, anticipation and fulfilment". These two, Fuad from Jerusalem, and Debby, from Tennessee, have teamed together and come up with a winner. The following recipes only hint at the rich assortment to be discovered at Chutneys.

APPETIZER
Marinated Rosemary Mozzarella
Serves Four

- 1 pound mozzarella cheese cut into half inch cubes
- juice of 2 fresh lemons
- ½ cup red wine vinegar
- ½ cup virgin olive oil
- 2 tablespoons brown sugar
- dash of salt and pepper
- 3 cloves garlic, diced fine
- 1 tablespoon capers, diced fine
- 1 small jalapeño pepper, seeded and diced fine
- 1 tablespoon rosemary or
- 4 sprigs fresh rosemary

Pound garlic, jalapeño, capers and salt and pepper in a bowl until a pulp forms. Add lemon juice, vinegar and brown sugar. Mix well. Add olive oil and mix. Add rosemary. Refrigerate overnight. When ready to serve, toss cheese into the mixture. Serve with crusty French or Italian bread.

MAIN COURSE
Chicken Saltimbocca With Marsala Wine
Serves Four

8	breasts of chicken boned and skinned, slightly pounded
4	slices very thinly sliced proscuitto ham
4	slices mozzarella cheese
2	tablespoons olive oil
2	tablespoons butter
1	clove garlic smashed and diced very fine
1	pound thinly sliced mushrooms
	salt and pepper to taste
	juice of one lemon
1/4	cup dry Marsala wine
	chopped fresh parsley for garnish

In a large copper skillet, melt butter and olive oil. Heat on medium burner. Add garlic and toss. Add lemon juice and wine and mix thoroughly. Add mushrooms and toss. Add chicken and cook three minutes on each side or until cooked. When chicken is ready, place one piece of ham and one piece of cheese on four of the chicken breasts. Top with other pieces of chicken and ladle juices over until cheese melts and binds the chicken breasts. Serve on a warmed plate. Garnish with chopped parsley.

Fresh Green Beans in Butter
Serves Four

32	tender fresh green beans, strings removed
2	tablespoons olive oil
2	tablespoons butter
	juice of one lemon
	salt and white pepper to taste
1/2	teaspoon thyme

Mix olive oil, butter, salt, pepper and thyme. Add lemon juice and mix. Add green beans and coat thoroughly with the mixture. On medium heat toss the beans in a skillet for a few minutes until tender. Serve with sprinkle of freshly ground black pepper.

DESSERT
Caramel Custard
Serves Four Plus

¾ cup sugar
3 eggs
   pinch salt
2 cups milk
½ teaspoon vanilla

Preheat oven to 300 degrees. In heavy skillet heat 1/2 cup sugar over medium heat stirring constantly until mixture turns a caramel color. Pour spoonful of syrup into four custard cups and let stand until cooled. Beat eggs slightly with remaining sugar and salt. Add milk slowly, while stirring. Add vanilla and strain. Pour strained mixture carefully into prepared cups. Place cups in baking dish and fill baking dish with water up to 1/2 inch below rims of custard cups.

Bake in preheated oven until a knife inserted into the center comes out clean, about 40 minutes. Remove from water and cool. Chill. To serve, run a knife around the edge of the custard, turn upside down onto plate and serve with whipped cream.

BEVERAGE
Cappuccino Brandy
Serves One

   Espresso coffee
¼ cup milk
1 teaspoon sugar
1 teaspoon cocoa
1 ounce brandy

Prepare coffee. Bring milk to boil; add sugar. Stir: Add cocoa. Stir: Add brandy. Stir: Add coffee. Top with whipped cream and a sprinkle of ground cinnamon. Serve with a thin wafer.

Bob Williamson

The Covey

Quail Lodge is a fine Carmel Valley resort on which the Mobil Travel Guide 5-star Award has been bestowed for 14 consecutive years. The superb cuisine at their Covey Restaurant reflects the resort's high standards. Chef Bob Williamson has won acclaim in the restaurant industry for his appealing menu and presentation in the resort's elegant dining room. The Englishman's experience at notable European restaurants brings to the menu a variety of international dishes. The restaurant is a favorite of locals and guests, who return again and again to The Covey Restaurant where Williamson caters to their every whim.

APPETIZER
Chilled Fried Scallops With Salsa
Serves Four

10 ounces large scallops
1 cup olive oil
3 whole Thai chilies (optional)
   flour, beaten egg and white bread crumbs
3 cloves garlic, split

Slice scallops into 1/4 inch thick slices. Season with salt and pepper. Bread scallops by dredging with flour, dipping in egg and rolling in bread crumbs.

Heat oil in a heavy skillet. Add garlic and chilies. Cook at medium temperature for 3-4 minutes to impart flavor to the oil. Do not burn. Discard garlic and chilies.

Fry scallops in flavored oil to a light golden brown. Chill. Serve with salsa.

Pasilla and Cilantro Salsa

1-1/2 cups diced tomato
1/4 cup chopped red onion
2 tablespoons chopped pasilla or jalapeño chilies
2 tablespoons lime juice
1 tablespoon chopped cilantro
   salt and pepper to taste

Place ingredients in bowl and stir.

SOUP
Split Pea Soup With Orange Sabayon

- 2 cups dried split peas
- 1 small onion
- 1 small leek
- 2 ounces butter
- 1 sprig thyme
- 8 cups good chicken stock
- 2 ribs celery
- 2 cloves garlic
- 1 small bay leaf
- 1 blade lemon grass
- salt and pepper to taste

Roughly dice vegetables. Heat butter in sauce pan. Add vegetables and cook gently in butter 4-5 minutes. Add peas and herbs. Add stock. Bring to boil. Cover, simmer 30-40 minutes stirring occasionally. Strain through cone shaped strainer, or process in food mill and then strain. Season to taste with salt and pepper. Pour into individual soup bowls and top with Orange Sabayon.

Orange Sabayon

- Chopped zest (rind of lemon) and juice of a medium orange
- 1/2 cup whipping cream (whipped)
- 2 egg yolks

Combine zest, juice and yolks in a stainless bowl. Place over boiling water (or your simmering pea soup) and whisk vigorously until the mixture will hold a peak. Remove from heat and allow to cool a little. Fold in whipped cream.

MAIN COURSE
Veal Dungeness
Serves Four

- 4 (4 oz.) medallions of veal loin (salt and pepper, flour)
- 2 ounces clarified butter
- 6 ounces Dungeness crab meat
- 6 ounces grated dry Monterey Jack cheese
- 1 tablespoon chopped shallot
- 1 tablespoon brandy

With a meat mallet and a not-too-heavy hand, flatten the veal to a thickness of approximately 1/4 inch. Season with salt and pepper and dust with flour.

Heat the butter in a heavy skillet and sauté veal on both sides. Do not overcook!

Arrange veal on a heatproof platter. Discard cooking fat and add chopped shallot to the skillet. Cook briefly. Add crab and heat through; add brandy and allow it to flame.

Arrange crab on top of the veal. Cover crab generously with grated cheese. Place under broiler until cheese starts to melt. Serve with pasta or gnocchi.

DESSERT
Peach and Almond Pie
Yields One Nine-Inch Pie

- 3 medium ripe peaches
- 4 ounces unsalted butter (room temperature)
- 3 ounces ground almonds
- 1 tablespoon sliced almonds
- 1 9-inch pie crust
- 5 ounces fine granulated sugar
- 2 eggs (room temperature)
- 1 ounce flour
- 1 tablespoon granulated sugar

Immerse peaches in boiling water for 30 seconds. Place in cold water, remove skin, cut in half. Remove pits and cut into six sections.

Cream butter and sugar together until sugar is thoroughly absorbed. Beat eggs and add to butter mixture a little at a time, beating well after each addition. Fold in ground almonds and flour.

Place half of the almond mixture in pie pan and arrange the peaches on it. Cover with rest of mixture. Sprinkle with sliced almonds and sugar. Bake at 375 degrees for 50 minutes or until our old friend the toothpick comes out clean. Serve with creme anglaise, whipped cream or ice cream.

BEVERAGE
Richard's Covey Coffee

- $1/3$ shot Chambord
- $1/3$ shot Gran Marnier
- $1/3$ shot Kahlua

Place in a 12 ounce stemmed glass. Fill to within one inch from the top with Colombian coffee. Top with fresh whipped cream.

Joe Zoellin

Flaherty's

There are two restaurants located side-by-side—one offers the ambience of a dinner house; the other has a more casual atmosphere just right for families and lighter fare. The marble counter makes a perfect lunch spot, and solo diners are sure to meet an interesting array of people. Chef Joe Zoellin enjoys specializing in seafood. "I was born in Carmel and always ate seafood as a kid. I'm lucky to be here where there is ample fresh produce; and the bounty from the ocean makes it easy to cook when everything is fresh."

APPETIZER
Ceviche Cocktail
Serves Eight

- 1/4 pound sole, cut in strips
- 1/4 pound small Bay scallops
- 1 large red onion, diced fine
- 1/4 cup tomato puree
- 1/4 cup tomato juice
- 1 teaspoon salt
- 16 stuffed green olives, sliced thin
- 2 tablespoons Worcestershire sauce
- 1 teaspoon Tabasco sauce
- 1/4 cup canned (Ortega) green chilies, chopped
- 3 tomatoes, peeled, seeded and chopped
- 2 tablespoons cilantro, chopped
- 1/4 pound small Bay shrimp, cooked

Cover sole and scallops with 2 cups lemon juice for 6 hours, in a glass bowl. When marinated, pour off half the liquid and add remainder of ingredients.

Mix well and refrigerate overnight. Serve in cocktail glass with wedge of lemon or lime.

SOUP
New England Clam Chowder
Serves Eight

4 ounces bacon ends and pieces	Process bacon ends in food processor until fine, then sauté in large heavy pot until fat is cooked out. Add diced celery and onions and cook until transparent. Add clam juice and seasonings. Bring to a boil. Meanwhile peel potatoes. Puree to a heavy mush. Add potatoes to boiling clam juice mixture and cook until thickened and potatoes are done. Remove from heat, stir in half-and-half and chopped clams.

- 4 ounces bacon ends and pieces
- 1/4 bunch celery, diced
- 1 large yellow onion, diced
- 3 cups clam juice
- 2 pounds baking potatoes
- thyme, black pepper, salt to taste
- 1 pint half-and-half
- 12 ounces chopped clams

Process bacon ends in food processor until fine, then sauté in large heavy pot until fat is cooked out. Add diced celery and onions and cook until transparent. Add clam juice and seasonings. Bring to a boil. Meanwhile peel potatoes. Puree to a heavy mush. Add potatoes to boiling clam juice mixture and cook until thickened and potatoes are done. Remove from heat, stir in half-and-half and chopped clams.

MAIN COURSE
Scampi Style Prawns Italiano
Serves Eight

- 48 large prawns, peeled and deveined
- flour for dredging
- butter, clarified
- 3 tablespoons freshly ground garlic
- 3 tablespoons freshly ground shallots
- 1 cup mushrooms, sliced
- 1/2 cup green onions, chopped
- 3 tablespoons capers, drained
- 16 black olives, pitted
- 16 artichoke hearts, canned non-marinated cooked and quartered
- 2 medium tomatoes, peeled and diced
- 1 tablespoon tomato paste
- 6 ounces white wine (Chablis)
- 1 cup clam juice

Dredge prawns in flour. Heat butter in sauté pan until hot. Place prawns in pan and cook on high heat until brown on one side. Turn and add wine, garlic, shallots, green onions and mushrooms. When wine has evaporated, add remaining ingredients and cook until sauce has reduced slightly. Serve over hot buttered pasta with fresh grated Parmesan cheese.

DESSERT
Brandy Apple Raisin Pie
Yields one ten inch pie

1	cup raisins
1	ounce brandy
3	quarts apple slices
1	cup super fine sugar
$1/3$	cup flour
1	teaspoon ground nutmeg
1	teaspoon ground cinnamon
	dash of salt

Soak raisins in brandy (overnight, if possible). Mix all dry ingredients together. Add raisins and dry mixture to apple slices. Mix well. Place in pastry lined pie pan. Top with brown sugar topping. Bake at 400 degrees until crust is brown and pie is bubbling about 45 minutes.

Brown Sugar Topping

$2/3$	cup flour
$1/2$	cup brown sugar
$1/4$	cup butter, firmly packed
1	teaspoon ground cinnamon
$1/2$	teaspoon ground cloves

Mix all ingredients until crumbly. Serve hot with ice cream or whipped cream.

Marc Vedrines

The French Poodle

The French Poodle is one of Carmel's great treasures. Its owner, Marc Vedrines, took over the already established restaurant in 1975 after a ten-year stint as executive chef at The Lodge at Pebble Beach. As the name would imply, classic French fare is served. In heavily accented English, the Frenchman states, "I like to work with food and I do it with love." The French Poodle has a faithful local following encouraged by the warm welcome from Marc's wife, Michele, who stays out of the kitchen because she is busy in the dining room. "I try to orchestrate the dining room to equate with the cuisine." These two take great pride in ensuring that the people who come there have a wonderful dining experience! Reserve early.

SOUP
Soupe de legumes (Vegetable Soup)
Serves Eight

- 2 onions, pared, chopped
- 2 leeks, white part only, washed, chopped
- 3 teaspoons olive oil
- 3 teaspoons sweet butter
- 2 celery ribs, chopped
- 4 tomatoes, ripe, peeled, diced
- 6 cups beef bouillon
- 2 carrots, chopped
- 3 medium potatoes, pared, raw
- 1/2 cup dry white wine
- 1 teaspoon parsley, minced
- 1 teaspoon basil, minced
- salt and pepper to taste

Sauté onions and leeks in olive oil and butter until soft. Add celery and tomatoes, cook until tomatoes are reduced and very soft. Add beef bouillon, carrots and potatoes and cook for 35 minutes, or until potatoes and carrots are very soft. Add wine.

Puree in blender or food processor. Garnish with parsley and basil.

MAIN COURSE
Filet de Veau en chemise
(Fillet of veal in pancake, tiny crepe)
Serves Eight

8 (3 oz.) veal fillets 6-8 tablespoons butter salt and pepper to taste	Sauté until browned and three-quarters cooked. Salt and pepper to taste. Remove veal and keep warm.
16 mushroom caps, sliced thinly 3-4 tablespoons shallots, pared, chopped finely	Sauté in pan for a few minutes.
2-3 ounces dry sherry 4 ounces veal stock	Add, cook while stirring, until reduced by half.
8 prepared crepes 3 ounces Gruyere cheese, grated	Spoon even part of mushroom and shallot mixtures on one side of each crepe. Place fillet on top and close crepe very carefully. Turn over, place on a buttered sheet pan. Brush melted butter over each crepe as needed. Sprinkle grated cheese over each crepe. Place in preheated 420 degree oven for 5-8 minutes.

DESSERT
Créme Renversee l'orange
(Custard with Orange Flavor)

- 1 quart of milk
- 1 dozen eggs
- 1-1/2 **cups sugar for caramel**
- 2 cups sugar
- 1 teaspoon vanilla extract
- 2 ounces Gran Marnier
- 2 oranges

Materials:
- 12 (8-ounce) ramequins
- 1 bain marie

Preheat oven to 420 degrees. In a small pan cook 1-1/2 cups sugar with 3/4 cup water to make a nice brown caramel. Once the caramel is ready, pour into individual ramequins.

In another pan, boil the milk with one teaspoon of vanilla extract. In a large bowl place 6 whole eggs and 6 yolks. Add 2 cups of sugar, plus 2 ounces of Gran Marnier and the juice of 2 oranges. Pour boiling milk over, pass through a sieve and pour 6 ounces of the preparation into the ramequins with some orange zest (rind). Bake in a bain marie (pan with water) for 40-45 minutes at 420 degrees.

Greg Cellitti

Friar Tuck's

You come to Friar Tuck's certainly for the food—scrumptious breakfasts, heavenly hamburgers and sundaes with ice cream and chocolate sauce piled high. You also come for the merriment. It is here that owner and chef, Greg Cellitti, holds court with his local following. They, along with many tourists, are engaged in light-hearted conversation throughout their meal and endless coffee refills provided by his long-time associate, Pam. It's all good fun. Since Carmelites do not receive home mail delivery, the Post Office continues to be a locals gathering place—look for Friar Tuck's next door.

SALAD

Hot Spinach Salad

Serves Four

- 1 pound fresh spinach
- 6-8 slices of bacon
- 1 cup French dressing
- 1/4 cup finely chopped onions
- 1/2 cup fresh mushrooms, chopped
- 1/2 cup raisins
- 1/4 cup grated Parmesan cheese
- 1 lemon

Trim roots and thick stems from spinach. Discard bruised leaves. Drop crisp leaves into large pan filled with warm water. Drain. Place in salad bowl and set aside.

In a 10 to 12 inch frying pan, cook bacon over medium heat until crisp. Lift bacon out, drain on paper towels, and set aside. Pour off and discard all but 4 tablespoons of the drippings. Add chopped onions to drippings in pan and stir over medium heat until lightly browned. Add French dressing and stir over high heat until it comes to a boil. Turn heat off and add crumbled bacon to dressing mixture.

Pour 3/4 of hot dressing over spinach and toss until well mixed. Place spinach mixture on individual serving plates. Top salad with remainder of dressing, mushrooms, raisins, grated cheese and sprinkle with lemon juice. Enjoy!!!

Scott Negri

Giuliano's

Diners who venture into Giuliano's are in for a treat. This is an intimate, elegant Northern Italian ristorante. Since 1981, Bob and Susan Negri have operated Giuliano's together with their sons. Michael is the maitre d' and Scott, at age 23, is undoubtedly the area's youngest chef. He began helping with food preparation in the family business when he was a teenager. "Yes," says the youthful Scott, "I've worked my way up in the kitchen; my Mom, a talented cook herself, is my main inspiration."

SALAD
Smoked Mozzarella and Tomato Salad
Serves Six

6 large tomatoes (6 slices per person)
1 pound smoked mozzarella cheese thinly sliced (5 slices per person)
Italian flat-leaf parsley, minced (for garnish)

Core and slice each tomato into 8 slices. Discard the end slices. Alternate tomato and mozzarella slices on six salad plates.

Drizzle each salad with dressing and dust with a bit of parsley.

San Remo Dressing

1/4 cup virgin olive oil
1/8 cup balsamic vinegar
1 tablespoon San Remo tomatoes (in jar), diced
2 teaspoons garlic, minced
2 teaspoons fresh basil, minced
2 teaspoons Parmesan cheese
fresh ground pepper

Whisk olive oil and vinegar together. Add tomatoes, garlic, basil, Parmesan cheese, and pepper to taste. Let dressing marinate at least 1/2 hour.

MAIN COURSE
Leg of Lamb in Balsamic Vinegar

- 1 (5-6 pound) leg of lamb
- 1/4 cup olive oil
- 1/4 cup balsamic vinegar
- 1/2 tablespoon dried rosemary, whole or twice that much, if fresh
- 2 garlic cloves, crushed
- 3 tablespoons Dijon mustard
- salt and pepper, freshly ground, to taste

Using a sharp-pointed knife or a pot fork, pierce the leg in several places and soak it for 5 hours in olive oil mixed with vinegar.

Place on a roasting rack and rub with salt, pepper, rosemary, mustard and garlic. Place a meat thermometer in thickest part of leg. Do not touch the bone. Bake at 325 degrees until the meat thermometer reaches 140 degrees (about 1-1/4 to 1-3/4 hours). Baste with marinade several times during roasting. Remove from oven. Let sit 1/2 hour before carving. The lamb will continue to cook a bit. Slice at the table.

Fried Zucchini With Almonds
Serves Six

- 1-1/2 pounds fresh zucchini, about 6 to 8 inches long
- 2 tablespoons oil
- 2 tablespoons butter
- 1/4 cup dry white wine
- 2 tablespoons lemon juice
- 1/2 teaspoon salt
- 1/2 cup slivered almonds

Wash and cut zucchini into 1/4 inch slices; sauté in oil and butter for 5 minutes, stirring frequently. Add wine, lemon juice, and salt; simmer for 5 minutes; add almonds and simmer 5 minutes longer. Transfer to a warm serving dish and serve hot.

DESSERT
Frutta Fresca Alla Giuliano
Serves Six

- 1 bunch fresh mint for garnish
- 1-1/2 pounds seedless green grapes
- 1-1/2 pounds seedless Red Flame grapes

- 1 pint whipping cream, stiffly beaten
- 1/2 cup Amaretti cookie crumbs
- 6 long stemmed balloon-shaped wine glasses

Remove grapes from stems. Rinse and dry grapes. Put in a bowl and mix. Cover and chill until serving time.

Fold Amaretti crumbs into whipped cream.

Place 1 cup chilled grapes in each glass. Top grapes with a large dollop of Amaretti cream. Garnish with mint sprig and serve.

Alan and Kati Lewis

La Boheme

La Boheme is a small, intimate restaurant owned by Alan and Kati Lewis for the past eleven years. The focus of this unusual restaurant is a fixed-price menu with the entree changing nightly. In addition to a creative menu, the Lewises provide the setting for a highly pleasurable evening. "For us," says Kati, "every night is different. The element of boredom doesn't exist. It is a very well-rounded experience to be sure." The Lewises' frequent trips to Europe afford them the opportunity to develop new and exciting recipes fresh from the European dining scene.

SOUP
Curried Carrot Soup
Serves Six

- 1 tablespoon unsalted butter
- ½ large onion, coarsely chopped
- 6 carrots, peeled and coarsely chopped
- 1 celery stalk, coarsely chopped
- 1 garlic clove, minced
- 2 tablespoons curry powder
- 8 cups chicken stock or canned chicken broth freshly ground black pepper and salt to taste
- 2 tablespoons chopped chives for garnish

In a 3-quart pot, melt the butter. Add chopped vegetables and garlic and sauté for 5 minutes over medium heat, stirring often. Add curry powder and cook for several minutes, stirring constantly. Do not allow the curry to burn. Add the stock, turn up the heat to high, and bring to a boil. Lower the heat and simmer, uncovered, for 30 minutes. Puree the soup in several batches in a food processor or blender and return to the pot. Season to taste.

To serve, reheat, if necessary, and pour into warmed soup bowls. Sprinkle with chives.

SALAD
Salade Garnie

We like to use a simple mixture of lettuce (red leaf and romaine) for our salads. You may wish to add a variety of other greens. Quantities of ingredients are not indicated and of course you may substitute or add as you desire.

2 heads lettuce; preferably 1 red and 1 romaine tomato wedges thinly sliced smoked ham thinly sliced Italian dry salami sliced Gruyere, or other cheese sliced large red onion whole black pitted olives minced parsley	Place washed and dried lettuce on a large serving platter. Dress lightly with the following dressing recipe. Arrange above ingredients on lettuce and sprinkle with parsley.

Italiano Dressing

$1/3$ cup soy oil $1/3$ cup red wine vinegar and water (equal parts) 2 whole tomatoes, blanched and peeled; or small can (4 oz.) whole peeled tomatoes 2 tablespoons tomato puree 1 large clove garlic, peeled $1/4$ cup red table wine 1 tablespoon fresh lemon juice 1 tablespoon Dijon mustard $1/2$ teaspoon oregano $1/4$ teaspoon dried dill $1/4$ teaspoon thyme salt and coarse ground pepper to taste	Blend all ingredients in food processor. Prepare in advance so the flavors may develop.

MAIN COURSE
Boeuf á la Ficelle
Serves Four to Six

This meat preparation is simple yet delicious and healthy since there is no excess fat. It may be served with some of the cooking broth and Dijon mustard or mild horseradish.

2-3	pounds of beef tenderloin in one piece
2	quarts veal stock or pot-au-feu broth

Trim and tie beef fillet securely with cotton string around both its length and width, leaving a long end attached for use in lifting the meat from the cooking pot.

Lower the beef into the center of the simmering stock or broth, suspending it in the liquid by tying the string to a long spoon and resting the spoon on either side of the pot. The beef should not touch the pot. Cook over high heat for a few minutes then lower the heat and simmer the meat until it is done. It should be perfectly rare on the inside and just colored by the broth on the outside. The cooking time is the same as for roasting a fillet: about 10 minutes per pound; a good-sized whole fillet will take 20 to 30 minutes.

To serve, remove string and slice the fillet in 1/2 to 3/4 inch slices.

Pommes Vapeur

2	pounds red skin potatoes, washed and cut into quarters
2	tablespoons unsalted butter
1	teaspoon dried oregano salt and freshly ground black pepper to taste

Steam potato quarters until tender. Melt butter with oregano and toss potatoes in butter mixture, while adding salt and pepper until evenly coated.

Brian Whitmer

Pacific's Edge

Situated on a cliffside, Pacific's Edge Restaurant at the Highlands Inn affords diners a breathtaking view of the Carmel coast. Here chef Brian Whitmer offers a rich culinary experience to match the dramatic view. Whitmer's superb regional menu highlights seasonality. "We use available local products as building blocks for our menu." Whitmer began his career as a chef in a fine restaurant in Kansas and then became the banquet chef at New York's Tavern on the Green. "I earned the position as chef at Montracht, which received a 3-star rating from the New York Times." Whitmer came to the attention of the Highlands Inn while he did consulting jobs in Los Angeles. Of his Carmel experience as executive chef, he says enthusiastically, "I love cooking and people."

APPETIZER
Dungeness Crab Appetizer
Serves Eight

- 2 fresh Dungeness crabs, cracked and cleaned
- 2 English cucumbers
- 4 Roma tomatoes
- 2 tablespoons chopped fresh chives
- 4 lemons
- 1/2 cup virgin olive oil
- salt and pepper to taste

Crack crab shells and remove all meat, each portion about 1-1/2 to 2 ounces.

Peel cucumbers and slice very thinly, 1/8-inch lengthwise. After slicing is completed, take tip of a sharp paring knife and follow the edge, cutting long, thin strips resembling spaghetti. Make a small cross-cut in the tip of the tomato. Remove stem end and blanch in boiling water. Remove, peel and cut into quarters. Take out core and seeds and cut into small even squares.

Juice lemons and slowly whisk into olive oil to make vinaigrette. Salt and pepper to taste.

Lightly toss cucumber spaghetti with lemon dressing. Divide onto four salad plates. Mound the crab in the center, sprinkle with tomato squares and chives, and then drizzle with a little extra dressing.

MAIN COURSE
Roast Chicken With Whipped Potatoes and Sweet Garlic
Serves Eight

- 4 (2-1/2 to 3 lb.) chickens (fryers)
- 15 large spinach leaves, washed
- 4 ounces fresh foie gras (domestic)
- 2 tablespoons butter
- 40 cloves of fresh garlic
- 1/2 cup of fresh (or frozen) baby peas

Remove breasts from both sides of chicken to yield 2 half-breasts with wings attached. Remove both thigh portions and take out the thigh bone. With a mallet, pound the thighs so they are 1/4 inch thick. (Your local butcher can easily do this procedure for you.)

Melt butter in skillet. Add spinach and cook just until wilted. Season with salt and pepper and place on towel to absorb moisture. Place spinach leaves on pounded chicken thighs, skin-side facing the table, just to cover meat. Place a piece of foie gras, cut just like a cigarette, in the middle. Roll up the pounded thigh so the foie gras is exactly in the middle, with the spinach wrapped around it. Tie the roulade with butcher twine twice, so the meat is tight.

SAUCE

- 1 litre of red wine
- 1 large onion
- 2 ribs celery
- 1 large carrot
- 4 bulbs garlic
- 2 bay leaves
- 2 litres water
- 1 bunch marjoram

Roast the 4 carcasses of the chickens in a 450 degree oven until golden brown. Halfway, add 2 onions, skin on, cut in half. Add 4 bulbs garlic, also cut in half, so they brown with the bones. Deglaze pan with red wine, transfer to stove top, and reduce by two-thirds. Add water, carrot and celery, cut in one-inch pieces. Add bay leaves and marjoram and simmer until reduced by one-half. Strain through fine sieve. Reserve.

WHIPPED POTATOES

4 Idaho potatoes
1/2 pound butter
1/4 cup milk
  salt and pepper

Boil 4 potatoes, cut in quarters, with 1 tablespoon butter and 1 teaspoon salt. When thoroughly cooked, approximately 10 minutes, remove from water. Pass through a food mill. With a rubber spatula whip vigorously 1/2 pound butter and 1/4 cup hot milk into potatoes until fluffy. Season with salt and pepper and set aside in a warm place covered with plastic.

GARNISH

Remove whole garlic cloves from husk, place in aluminum foil, drizzle with olive oil and bake for 45 minutes until soft and golden. Cook peas in salted, boiling water until tender (approximately five minutes). Remove and cool in ice water to retain bright green color.

TO SERVE

Season chicken breasts and thighs with salt and pepper. In a heated skillet, place one tablespoon of olive oil, chicken and sauce, (skin side down on the breast), and sauté until golden on both sides. Place in 400 degree oven for five minutes on the breasts and 10 minutes on the thighs. Remove from oven and let rest. Cut string of thighs. Arrange a small mound of whipped potatoes on middle of plate, place chicken breast in front, tucked into potatoes, and the thigh, cut into three "medallions" facing up, tucked behind the potatoes. Drizzle 1 ounce of sauce over meat, and sprinkle re-warmed peas and 5 garlic cloves around plate.

Remo d'Agliano

Raffaello

Remo d'Agliano is the chef/owner of Raffaello. He is well prepared to operate his fine North Italian-style restaurant. From the early age of 45 days, Remo was in the kitchen with his chef father. Remo's career took him to many countries from his native Florence—France, Switzerland, England and Scotland—before he accepted the position as manager of Pebble Beach's Club XIX. For 25 years, since that time, Remo has owned and operated the cozy Raffaello Restaurant, where he and his mother, Amelia, work as a team.

MAIN COURSE
Vitella Primavera
Serves Four

4	slices veal filet, pounded until thin
4	garlic cloves, chopped
8	cups tomatoes, peeled and chopped
4	slices Fontina cheese
1	teaspoon oregano, fresh or dried
4	teaspoons Worcestershire sauce
2	tablespoons fresh parsley, chopped
1/4	cup Parmesan cheese
	olive oil
	salt and pepper to taste

Heat olive oil. Add veal slices. Salt, pepper and fry on both sides until brown.

In a separate pan, sauté the garlic in olive oil. Add tomatoes and oregano. Salt and pepper, reduce heat and cook slowly for five minutes.

Add meat juices to tomato mixture. Add Worcestershire sauce.

Place a slice of Fontina cheese on each veal slice and pour small amount of sauce over the top. Cook for five more minutes. Press remaining sauce through a seive. Add the parsley.

When the veal is ready to serve, sprinkle with Parmesan cheese and brown for two minutes. Serve sauce separately.

Bill Huneke

Rio Grill

Rio Grill, one of the area's most popular restaurants, draws in locals by the dozens. It's a meeting place, a place to relax with friends over drinks or lunch or dinner. The self-taught chef, Bill Huneke, from Sonoma, got sidetracked from his Ag major in school, and he says, "I ended up working in a lot of different restaurants." The Rio Grill menu is packed with innovative dishes. A small sampling of the chef's delightful creations is included here.

SALAD
Watercress, Orange-lemon Salad
Serves Six

- 4 oranges
- 4 lemons
- 2 cherry tomatoes
- 3 ounces bleu cheese, crumbled
- 1/4 cup walnuts toasted
- 4 large bunches of watercress, large stems trimmed

Cut the peel and all the white pith from the oranges and lemons. Cut crosswise into 1/4 inch thick slices and remove seeds.

Toss watercress, walnuts and cherry tomatoes with half of vinaigrette. Arrange watercress onto 6 chilled salad plates. Arrange tomatoes, walnuts, lemon and orange slices throughout salad. Drizzle remaining vinaigrette over salads and top with bleu cheese crumble.

Black Pepper Citron Vinaigrette

- 1 cup mild olive oil
- 1/2 cup fresh orange juice
- 1/4 cup fresh lemon juice
- 2 tablespoons coarsely ground pepper
- salt to taste

Mix ingredients together.

MAIN COURSE
Grilled Swordfish With Avocado Papaya Salsa
Serves Six

- 6 (6 oz.) pieces of swordfish loin

Gently combine all salsa ingredients. Use within 2 hours since salsa will begin to break up after that.

Grilling Mixture

- ½ cup mild olive oil
- 1 tablespoon chopped garlic
- salt and pepper to taste
- 1-½ cups of avocado papaya salsa

Preheat barbecue grill. Lightly brush swordfish with olive oil mixture and sprinkle with salt and pepper to taste. Grill until medium rare, about 4 minutes per side, turning once.

Salsa

- 4 ripe papayas peeled, seeded and medium diced
- 4 avocados peeled, seeded and medium diced
- 3 tablespoons finely diced red onion
- ⅛ teaspoon of red chili flakes
- 3 tablespoons fresh lime juice
- 3 tablespoons sour cream

Divide salsa among 6 warm dinner plates and serve swordfish on top of sauce.

DESSERT
Jack Daniel's Chocolate Ice Cream
Serves Six

- 1 cup sugar
- 3 cups cream
- 3 cups half-and-half
- 1/2 cup Dutch cocoa powder
- 9 egg yolks
- 1/2 cup Jack Daniel's bourbon

In sauce pan combine cream, half-and-half and dutch cocoa powder. Slowly whisk to ensure there are no lumps. Heat to a simmer. Remove from heat.

Whisk sugar and egg yolks together until smooth and sugar is dissolved. Slowly add 1/3 of cream mixture to egg yolks stirring all the time. Slowly add yolks and remaining cream, continue to stir. Return to heat and slowly stir until cream will coat the back of a spoon. Remove from heat. Add bourbon and stir.

Chill before placing in ice cream freezer. Follow the directions for the ice cream freezer.

Peter Oda

Robata Grill

Approach Robata through The Barnyard, a rustic shopping area replicating barns of an earlier era. Once inside the Japanese restaurant, you'll find surroundings of dark wood, ornate straw sake cases, bamboo and straw basket lanterns. Dining is intimate in the partitioned booths, or lively at the long redwood bar behind whch meals are prepared on an open grill. Here you find Chef Peter Oda, known as Odasan, where he's been since Robata opened 10 years ago. Odasan's restaurant career spans fifty years. He has owned restaurants in Minnesota and in Monterey. "I retired once for two years, but I like people too much to stay home." And people like Odasan and his cooking too much to stay away from Robata.

MAIN COURSE
Clam Foil Yaki

This dish is designed to be prepared Robata yaki style (on your barbecue).

1	pound fresh Manilla clams
1/2	cup sake
1	tablespoon soy sauce
2	cloves garlic, minced
1/2	cube butter
1	teaspoon salt
1	large piece aluminum foil
1	wedge lemon

Double up on aluminum foil to make an 18 x 18 inch square. Slightly fold up all edges so you won't lose any sake.

Place the clams in the center. Add the rest of the ingredients. Pull up the edges and seal. Place complete foil pouch on the barbecue. In 7-10 minutes peek in the foil. If the clams are open, place the foil pouch in a bowl. Fold back foil and serve with a wedge of lemon.

Jean Hubert

Sans Souci

The French name means "without worry", and this is a place where cares disappear under the auspices of owners John Jay and Cindykay Williams. It is a cozy, intimate French restaurant. Chef Jean Hubert has garnered a top reputation at Sans Souci where the style of cooking is classic or nouvelle. Hubert grew up in Santa Cruz and learned his French cooking flair from his father. "He gave me my enthusiasm," he says. Hubert gained experience at what he calls the true culinary capital of France—Lyon—where he worked at Vettard, a top restaurant. Hubert has also worked in some of San Francisco's better French restaurants. To Hubert, working as a chef is more than a job. "It's my calling—I truly enjoy what I do."

APPETIZER
Abalone
Serves Four

1 large pink abalone (shucked, trimmed and flattened)
1 large egg (beaten)
  flour
  juice of 2 lemons
4 tablespoons sweet butter
  salt and white pepper

Season abalone steaks. Lightly flour both sides. Dip in beaten egg. Cook in large skillet in very hot butter or oil. Let steaks become brown. If cooked too long, they will become tough. Remove abalone to warm plate. Add lemon juice to skillet. Then add butter and whip until creamy. Serve over top of abalone and garnish with lemon crown or wedge.

MAIN COURSE

Fillet of Salmon With Black and Gold Chantrelles
Serves Four

- 2 pounds of fresh salmon fillet (cut into 4 equal portions)
- 1/2 pound each of black and gold chantrelle mushrooms (or substitute button mushrooms)
- 1/4 cup of cream
- 1/4 cup fume (fish stock) or substitute clam juice
- 1-2 minced shallots
- salt and white pepper

Place salmon fillets in buttered baking dish. Cover fillets with mushrooms, cream shallots and fish fume. Cover dish with aluminum foil or close fitting top. Bake for 15 to 20 minutes at 450 degrees. Remove salmon/mushroom mixture to a sauce pot. Reduce until thick enough to stand upon the fish. Season with salt and white pepper and cover fish fillets. Garnish with fresh herbs.

Gratin Potatoes

- 4 pounds potatoes peeled, sliced as thinly as possible
- 1 cup of cream
- 2 cloves of fresh garlic, minced
- 1/8 teaspoon salt
- 1/8 teaspoon white pepper
- dash nutmeg

Place sliced potatoes in a bowl. Cover with cream, add garlic then seasonings. Place potatoes in a gratin or other casserole dish. Pour cream mixture over them. Bake for 2-1/2 hours at 200 degrees.

DESSERT
Chocolate Raspberry Pâté

- $3/4$ **pound dark semi-sweet chocolate**
- $1/4$ **pound cream cheese, softened**
- 4 **tablespoons softened sweet butter**
- $1/8$ **cup milk**
- 3 **eggs separated**
- $1/8$ **cup granulated sugar**
- $1/2$ **pint of fresh raspberries**

In a bowl melt chocolate in a double-boiler with milk. In a separate bowl add sugar to egg yolks and beat until very fluffy. In a separate bowl whip egg white until fluffy. When chocolate is melted add the fluffy yolk mixture and whip until smooth. Add butter a tablespoon at a time until blended. Now fold the egg whites and pour into mold. Let chill. In another bowl, hand mix 1/2 of raspberries with cream cheese until smooth. When pâté is cold, unmold by warming loaf pan in warm water. Garnish with cream cheese and remaining raspberries.

Bryan Carr

Spyglass

Bryan Carr comes from a small town in the Missouri Ozarks that, he says, "no one has ever heard of." He became a cook in Santa Barbara because he needed a job. Through hard work, Carr has moved into the executive chef position at one of Carmel's oldest and finest establishments, where he has performed for the past year and a half. About La Playa, Carr remarks, "The building and grounds are really unique. From the outdoor terrace, you can hear the ocean, while inside the light changes constantly. It is a great setting for cooking." And a great setting for eating the Spyglass's contemporary California/French fare. La Playa's gardens and vista of Carmel's beautiful surroundings make this a favorite for residents and return visitors.

SALAD
Scallop Salad with Warm Hazelnut Vinaigrette
Serves Four

- 20 pieces sea scallops
- 1 handful hazelnuts, toasted and peeled*
- 1 tablespoon ground coriander seeds**
- 4 ounces hazelnut oil
- 1-2 ounces good quality white wine vinegar
- lettuce enough for four salads

Choose a selection of lettuce varieties or include greens, such as turnip tops or mustard greens. Spinach and endive are also very good in this salad. Clean lettuce, mix, dry thoroughly and reserve.

Heat a sauté pan until very hot. Pour one ounce oil into pan and, working quickly so the oil has no chance to burn, place scallops in oil. Large scallops are easiest to work with. Cook scallops for about 45 seconds on one side, reducing the heat if the oil starts to smoke. Shake the pan gently to ensure the scallops do not stick. Turn scallops to cook the other side. Add hazelnuts and coriander and cook for 45 seconds. Add a small dash of vinegar and shake the pan so all the scallops are covered with both oil and vinegar. Remove scallops from pan and hold in a warm place.

-continued-

Scallop Salad (continued)

Remove pan from heat and taste the mixture it contains. This will be the dressing for your salad. If the vinegar taste is too strong, whisk in more oil. Season with salt and white pepper.

Divide the salad mix among four plates and put five warm scallops on each salad. Pour warm dressing over the salads and serve immediately. Work quickly and serve immediately so there is no chance of over-cooking the scallops.

*Place nuts in oven until dark brown. Remove and allow to cool. Rub hazelnuts between your hands to remove the thin husks.

**If you can't buy ground coriander simply place coriander seeds in a blender to grind them.

MAIN COURSE
Chicken and Sausage Cassoulet With Prosciutto

The cassoulet is a traditional country dish from the Southwestern region of France. Almost every culture, though, has at least one variation on this theme. In America beans with hamhocks is a delicious representative. You will use this recipe best if you try several different types, depending on your taste and what you have available. Here is an example to get you started.

1	chicken, meat removed from the bones
3	knockwurst sausages
4	slices prosciutto ham, trimmed of fat and cut into thin strips
20	ounces flageolets beans*
4	cups chicken stock
2	teaspoons chopped garlic
2	teaspoons chopped rosemary
2	teaspoons chopped sage
1	onion chopped
2	tomatoes, seeded and chopped
1	tablespoon tomato paste
1	cup white wine
4	ounces olive oil

*These French style beans can be bought cooked in cans.

Heat a large, heavy bottomed pot. When it is medium hot, pour in olive oil. Give the oil a moment to heat then drop in the chopped onion. Cook onion, stirring frequently, until it begins to soften. Add chicken and sausages, cut into large chunks—remember this is a country dish, not something fancy. Add ham. Cook the meats in the onions and oil for 4-5 minutes. Add rosemary, sage and garlic. Do not allow onions or garlic to brown; burning the garlic will ruin the dish. Cook all the ingredients mentioned above for 3-4 minutes then add tomato paste, cook for a minute or two and add chopped tomatoes.

You will now have the beginnings of your cassoulet. Pour in the wine to moisten all your ingredients. Give the wine a moment to do its work then add the chicken stock. At this point, add the beans and chicken stock.

Reduce the heat until you achieve a slow simmer and let your ingredients cook together for 30 minutes or more. This dish is particularly suited for a dinner party because you can proceed to this step hours–or even a day–in advance. When you are ready to serve give the cassoulet a few turns from the pepper mill, adjust the salt and divide among four hot soup bowls. Serve with a good warm bread and one of your favorite fresh vegetables on the side.

Aleen Hillbun

Tuck Box

Without a doubt, The Tuck Box English Tea Room is one of Carmel's most popular restaurants, whether folks come to photograph the delightful Comstock designed "Hansel and Gretel" house or to sample the popular scones. Tuck Box history dates back to the 1940's and the menu has changed little since then. The Hillbun family purchased the tiny cottage in 1976, though owner/chef Aleen Hillbun had been employed there since 1960. Even after 30 years, the convivial Hillbun will not divulge the scone recipe, but here are other Tuck Box treats in keeping with their credo: "The secret to the success of The Tuck Box has always been simple food prepared well."

Tuck Box Fruit Salad Dressing

1 cup mayonnaise
1/2 cup reserved fruit juice from salad
1/2 cup whipped cream

Mix mayonnaise and fruit juice well. Fold in whipped cream. Serve salad in individual bowls and top with dressing.

Nut bread is a nice complement.

MAIN COURSE
Tuck Box Meat Loaf

3 pounds ground beef
2/3 cup Quaker 5 minute oats
1/4 medium onion, grated
1 egg
  dash Tabasco sauce
2 tablespoons Worcestershire sauce
  enough tomato juice so the meat mixture does not hold its own shape.
  pinch of salt

Preheat oven to 350 degrees.

Place meat mixture in standard loaf pan and top with a thin layer of tomato juice.

Bake for approximately 1 hour. Serve with your favorite brown gravy.

Wine Tasting

With its lush rolling mountain hillsides and fresh ocean breezes, warm mornings and cool afternoons, Monterey County ranks among the finest wine growing regions in the world. Over 35,000 acres in vineyards makes Monterey County the largest coastal region in California. Superior grapes produce superior wine, and the remarkable grapes grown in this region are distinctive for their unusual fruitiness, well developed color and good sugar-acid balance which is responsible for the true, clear taste of each grape variety.

As its largest producer of varietal wines, the name Paul Masson is synonymous with Monterey wine country. The Paul Masson Wine Tasting Room, gift shop and museum is located on historical Cannery Row in Monterey. Commanding a spectacular view of Monterey Bay, the Tasting Room offers free wine tasting as well as fine premium varietal wines by the glass, bottle or case. The unique Museum of California Wine History boasts a fascinating collection of memorabilia, antique tools, winemaking implements and photographs. The museum is the only one of its kind anywhere. An extraordinary 10 minute film chronicles the career of Paul Masson and history of California wine making. The gift shop is truly a delight with a selection of fine gifts and gourmet food items from around the world.

The Paul Masson Wine Tasting Room, 700 Cannery Row, Monterey CA 93940

For additional copies fill out the order form below and mail to:

**A Taste of Carmel
P.O. Box 2213
Carmel CA 93921**

**Dealer inquiries welcome
Call (408) 624-4890**

---- ✂ ----

YES, I want to order____copies of **A TASTE OF CARMEL** at **$14.95** per copy
(California residents add $1.01 sales tax) plus $2.50 for shipping and handling.

My check, payable to
A TASTE OF CARMEL,
in the amount of $_____ is enclosed.

NAME _____

ADDRESS _____

CITY _____ STATE _____ ZIP _____

PHONE _____

Notes